For games, links and more, visit our interactive Web site: www.winslowpress.com

Library of Congress catalog card number: 98-89829
Printed in Hong Kong   First edition, 1999

WINSLOW PRESS

Designed by Bretton Clark and Billy Kelly

The ALPHABET Atlas

For Helene and Jerry

A.Y.   A.Y.

For Garvin

J.W.

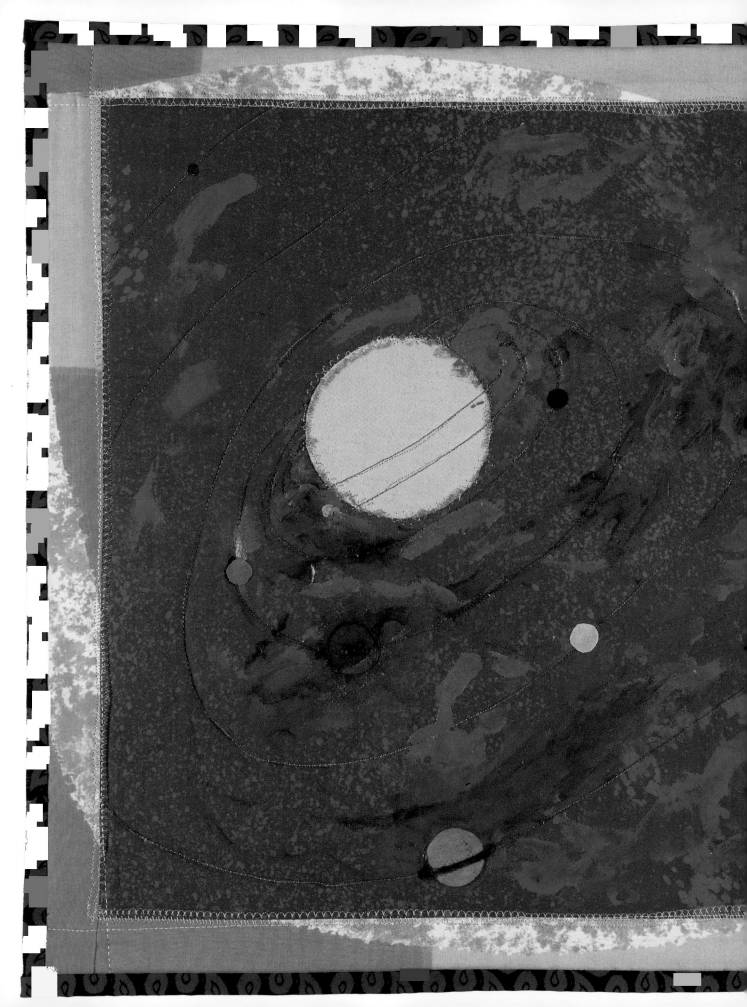

The ALPHABET Atlas

Arthur Yorinks

Illustrated by
Adrienne Yorinks

Letter Art by
Jeanyee Wong

WINSLOW PRESS

Australia is the flattest country in the world and
the only nation that is also a continent.

Brazil is home to the world's largest tropical rainforest.

C

Canada is very
big and has over thirty
thousand lakes.

Denmark, a farming country, is made up
of over four hundred islands.

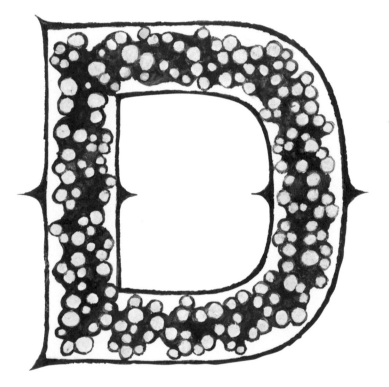

E

Egypt,
where the Nile River
runs, is the site of one of
the first civilizations on earth.

France has more people visit it than any other
country in the world.

Greece, with its thousands of islands, is where

democracy and the Olympics were born.

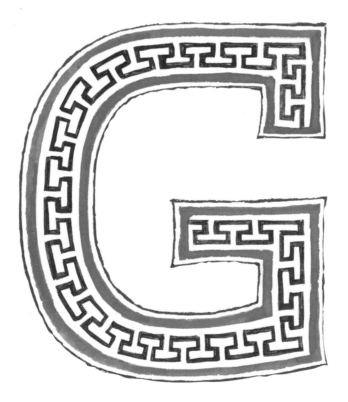

Haiti is the second oldest independent
country in the Americas.

India
has more
people than
every country
except China.

Japan, mainly comprised of four islands, has a lot
of volcanoes, including Mt. Fuji.

K

Kenya lies astride the equator, and many scientists think it is where the first human beings lived.

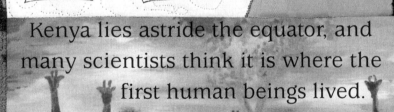

Luxembourg has many castles,

so many, in fact, that it is sometimes called the

"land of haunted castles."

M

Mexico was
once the land of the
great Aztec and
Mayan civilizations.

New Zealand is home

to about three and a half million people

and almost fifty million sheep.

Oman is mostly barren except for its oil,

but on its narrow plain,

dates, limes, and bananas are grown.

Portugal
is famous for its
almond trees,
and it

also
supplies
much of the
world's
cork.

P

Qatar is mostly a flat desert
with almost no vegetation, but it has lots of oil
and even more natural gas.

R

Russia is the largest country in the world and sent the first person into outer space.

South Africa has the world's most
diverse wildlife, with over one hundred thirty
species of mammals and over four hundred
and fifty species of birds.

Thailand, once called Siam,

produces more rice than any other country.

United States of America, where the United Nations is headquartered, is home to the world's oldest living thing: a bristlecone pine tree.

Venezuela is home to the

highest waterfall in the world, Angel Falls.

Wales is a part of the United Kingdom,

and it was in 1282 that Edward I began the custom of calling

the king's eldest son the Prince of Wales.

Xianggang (Hong Kong), a region
with many islands, was leased from China by
the British for ninety-nine years and now belongs
to China once again.

Yemen, once part of the ancient
Kingdom of Sheba, has many interesting structures such
as the pillars of the Awwam temple in Ma'rib.

Z

Zimbabwe,
crisscrossed
by many rivers,
is home to
the spectacular
Victoria Falls.

Author's Note

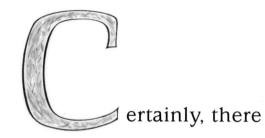

Certainly, there
is much to learn about the countries around the world.
This atlas gives you one or two facts about each country,
but there are many, many more. To delve deeper into the
history and culture of each region mentioned, please join
us at the wonderful Winslow Press Web site:
www.winslowpress.com.

Letterer's Note

In order to design
the letters for this alphabet, I found it essential to
live with and study the magnificent quilts by Adrienne,
creating letters that complemented the spirit and beauty
of each quilt. Enjoy.

Illustrator's Note

The illustrations in this book were made from many different fabrics, quilted, and turned into textile art. Where possible, I chose fabrics from the countries that are depicted. For example, in Kenya, note the brownish coarse fabric with X's. This is called mud cloth, and it is only created in Africa. Sometimes, the motifs within the fabrics used tell us something about the region itself. Look at the cowrie shells in Zimbabwe. These shells were important for trade before other currency existed. For more information on the illustrations and to see the countries in this atlas on a world map, visit the Winslow Press Web site at: www.winslowpress.com.

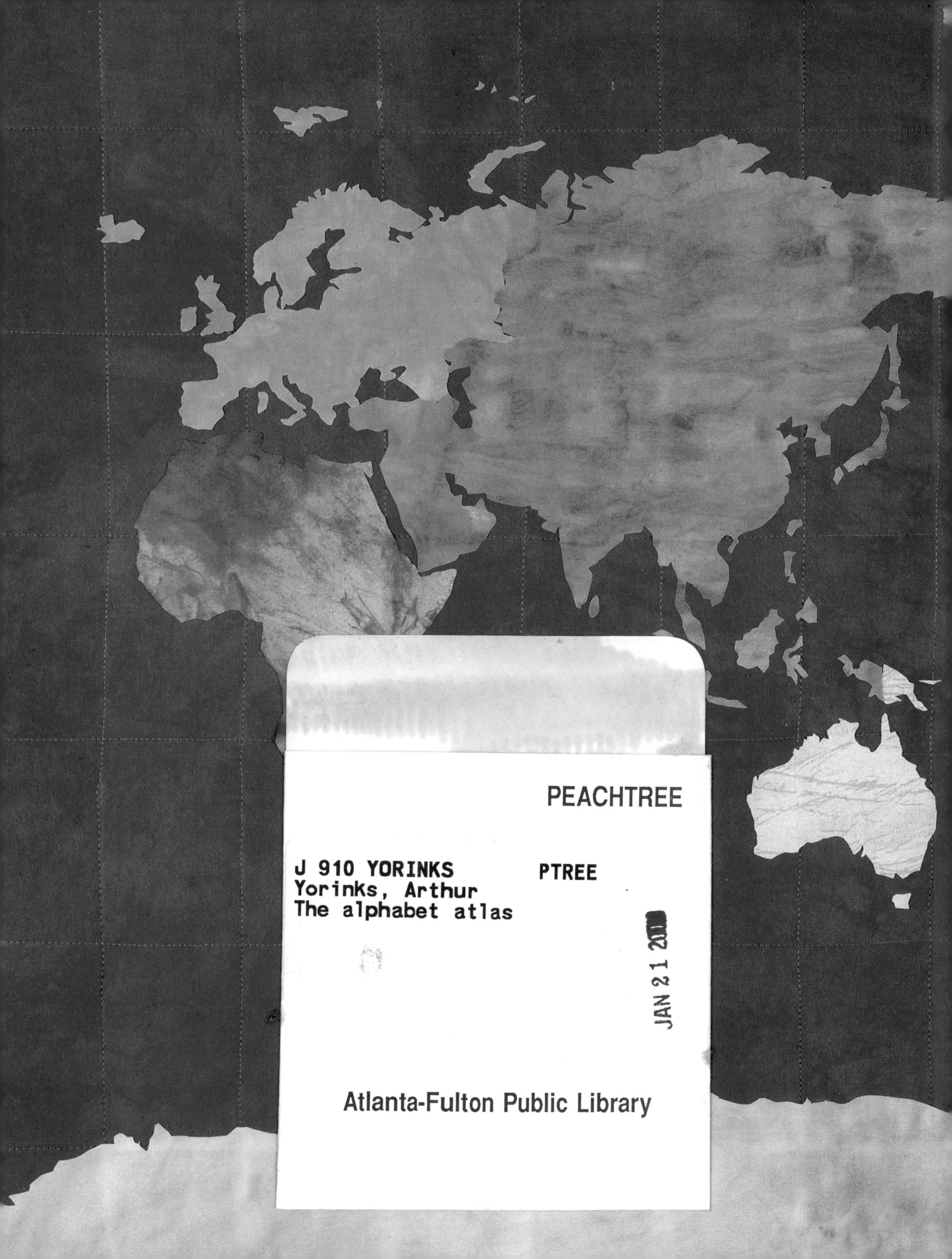